Gomer's Song

Gomer's Song

Kwame Dawes

BLACK GOAT
LOS ANGELES

BLACK GOAT is an independent poetry imprint of Akashic Books created and curated by award-winning Nigerian author Chris Abani. Black Goat is committed to publishing well-crafted poetry and will focus on experimental or thematically challenging work. The series aims to create a proportional representation of female, African, and other non-American poets. Series titles include:

Auto Mechanic's Daughter by Karen Harryman
eel on reef by Uche Nduka

Also by Kwame Dawes

Poetry
Resisting the Anomie
Progeny of Air
Prophets
Jacko Jacobus
Requiem
Shook Foil
Mapmaker
Midland
New and Selected Poems
Bruised Totems
I Saw Your Face
Wisteria: Twilight Songs from the Swamp Country
Brimming
Impossible Flying

Anthologies
Wheel and Come Again: An Anthology of Reggae Poetry (editor)
Twenty: South Carolina Poetry Fellows (editor)

Fiction
She's Gone
A Place to Hide and Other Stories

Nonfiction
Natural Mysticism: Towards a New Reggae Aesthetic
Talk Yuh Talk: Interviews with Anglophone Caribbean Poets
Bob Marley: Lyrical Genius
A Far Cry from Plymouth Rock: A Personal Narrative

Published by Akashic Books
©2007 Kwame Dawes

ISBN-13: 978-1-933354-44-6
Library of Congress Control Number: 2007926132
First printing

Black Goat
c/o Akashic Books
PO Box 1456
New York, NY 10009
info@akashicbooks.com
www.akashicbooks.com

For Lorna,
Sena, Kekeli, and Akua

And for
Mama the Great
Gwyneth, Kojo, Aba, Adjoa, and Kojovi

Remembering
Neville

Acknowledgments

These poems make no effort to retell the story of Gomer, the harlot wife of the prophet Hosea in the biblical book bearing his name. However, they imagine the psychological complexity of Gomer and find some mythic anchoring in that narrative.

Grateful acknowledgment to the following spaces: Cassava Piece, Kingston; Toronto, Canada; and Sumter, South Carolina. Thanks to Chris Abani, Johnny Temple, Colin Channer, Charlene Spearen, Donna Weir Soley, and Patricia Smith. Thanks also to the English Department at the University of South Carolina for the space to write, and to the staff for their patience and encouragement.

CONTENTS

III.

I

Hamilton, Ontario, 2002

"My nerves are bad to-night. Yes, bad. Stay with me.
"Speak to me. Why do you never speak. Speak.
"What are you thinking of? What thinking? What?
"I never know what you are thinking. Think."

—from *The Waste Land* by T.S. Eliot

ON ME AND MEN

1

Here is the calculus of desire —
I have studied its insides

like I have studied the language
of the sky. Sometimes before a storm,

I feel the wash of power when I face
the growing clouds, as if I have called

them all into being — the first flicker
of rain, an affirmation of my stomach's

command. It is the same with lust —
the way I plant seeds around me,

my arms, an arc of firm brown limbs
scattering the hint of possibility.

2

A man is calibrated to bore in —
wide open doors unnerve him, fluster

him. So just the hint of red panties,
or the whispered query: *Do you sleep*

in socks?—sometimes those are enough.
The rest is the ruse of silence,

the ordering of the elements,
the making of storms out of breeze.

He will ask me about other dreams
if I tell him of the dream of the wood-

cutter and the forest and my fear,
if I tell him I sweated and could not sleep,

if I say I would have wanted,
at that moment, to call someone;

he will ask me to dream again
tonight, and call him this time.

3

When, after a week, he is grunting
over me—startled at the suck

of my body, at the impossible
of his luck—he won't know

how easily we arrived here,
playing beasts in the half light;

won't know that I have washed
these sheets today, and will again

tonight; won't know that I ruin love
with a medley of men, slipping

into the soft hunger of my dreams;
won't know that I can make storms

and quiet them
with just a breath.

THE SINNER

A man who is just looking for companionship
is confused—one of those ordained types
who have not learned to live through nights
without a sermon to preach, and a hand to hold
along dark roads to cut with headlights
coming from the giddy flame of revival—
the kind who starts with questions,
wants to know what I do, where I am from,
wants to make conversation. And I listen,
waiting for his conscience to evaporate,
and then if I feel merciful, I say,
*I have my fingers in me, your voice
is making me wet*—and he laughs as if in shock;
and I say, *Are you shocked?*
Because he wants to be in shock, and then,
he finds the language of his heart,
words tumbling out, until he is uttering
in tongues, the music of his fallenness.
And after, he wants to pray for me,
wants to turn this into something
biblical, turn me into a scriptural whore
like that married seductress standing in her doorway
in Proverbs, someone ripe for healing.
He weeps because, you know,
all he wanted was companionship,
and because he just does not know

why he lets women do this to him,
especially since he loves his wife,
especially since he feels his sin heavy
on him all the time — it's never easy,
and he wants me to say I am sorry
for leading him astray;
he wants me to say I will pray with him.
You know that type, right?
Mostly, I tell them to go fuck themselves.

NUMBER FORTY-TWO

He says
his name is Rupert.

He has a voice
like an oily sardine tin.

He says
he has no skin cream.

He gets blisters.

He says *Jesus* with a Texan accent
when he comes.

GARDENING

Tonight I want a voice to crawl over me,
to say ordinary things, to stop

the quarrelling of my children,
to stop the racing in my head.

I tell him to read the newspaper to me,
The Home and Garden section, slowly.

I reach deep into me, feel the wet
of mud on my fingers. His voice is far,

a mess of gardenias, azaleas, compost,
and worms all around me.

I come smelling the brown scent
of warm broken soil.

WHILE WATCHING LETTERMAN

He says, *Say* yes *every time it goes in*
and no *every time it goes out.*
I say *yes* and *no*, waiting for him,

while Letterman with his bad teeth
and thinning hair does his stand-up.

I don't push it in and out;
my hand weighs like a rag
on my mound.

I wager he will be a squealer.
Waiting to hear distracts me.

He squeals, then asks, *You came?*
I lie. Letterman is making me laugh,
on the TV, so I laugh some more,
and tell him, *Yes, no, yes, no* . . .

BULLY-RIDER

A shy man is an excuse to call it off.
Instead I laugh at him, to his face,

reminding him of his boasts,
the lie he told of his dick's size,

the girlish perk of his breasts,
the cocky narrative of what he promised to do.

He stares back like a preschool bully
caught out, about to cry, and I reach

for the soft of his belly, poke it,
call him a slob, pushing him back,

looming over him, daring the little
lump not to grow, while I grind out my orgasm —

an irritating headiness, my mouth full
of cursing and gloating laughter.

REPENTANCE

First there is the wrenching of the body,
the pain of repeating this sweetness,
everything tender to the touch,
my head filled with sharp blue sky,
the sun relentless — a startling bomb each time.

Then the blood begins to return
to stiffened limbs, and the room grows
curry yellow before the brown
of regret. In this hiatus, I am clean
as a confessor, able again to rebuild
that new fiction of redemption.

And sated like this, it is easy
to say this will be the last
faceless man's basic desire,
the last pathetic stranger
to seep into me; that tomorrow
a new woman will begin
to rebuild the wreckage of her life.

For the hour rocking on the crosstown
late-night transit bus, empty
but for the dozing night people,
I am pure as repentance.

At sunrise, the hunger begins again,
and my blank page hungers
to be stained with new sordid epics.

FRESH

Lately my head don't feel like me.
I speak with a fake Yankee accent.
I learnt it from the giggly come-ons
of porn stars — I can't say *cunt*,
fuck, *cock*, *pussy* without faking
the slur of a stranger's tongue.
But this boy smells the earth
in the way my *H*s lose their way.
He says to me, laughing softly,
Say it like you would say it
where you come from,
I mean use your language;
it's nice, really nice.
So I say *pumpum* and *buddy*
and *battyhole* and I, too,
am fourteen, bare-thighed
behind the rum bar
under a sheltering breadfruit tree
with Danny saying, *It sweet,*
it sweet, it sweet . . .
And the boy likes to say *nice*,
and he whispers into the phone:
If you don't tell I am fourteen
I won't call the INS. And I know
the taste of sin: the pure light
of a soft boy's smile, the sound

of it growing with the shock
of his orgasms as if he will never
feel this again. And in the dark
I rock my body like prayer.
I am all water now,
praying for mercy on my soul.
Let's do it again, he says,
as if we are playing catch
or leaping off a cliff into a river.

BUSINESS CLASS

He says red wine and Italian
and we can make jokes and keep each other calm.

He says orgasms are antidepressants, something
about the brain. He sounds like a televangelist.

He sounds safe.
He is white, with brown eyes.

I lie to my husband, say I have to see my girlfriend
who is depressed by marital woes.

I eat little, drink quickly, and we walk
in the dark deep of the park.
My eyes will not focus.

Desire is a vague equation here,
the air on my bare thigh feels clean.

His hair is tidy, looks like a businessman —
is careful to hang his jacket, remove his ring.

I think of his voice on the phone,
its quiet efficiency, as he turns his fingers

deep in me. He calls another woman's name
when he spills himself into my cupped palm.

NAME

And there is silence —
I hear the rustle of paper,
the polite clearing of his throat.

He knows what I am doing,
hears the stifling of my breath,

Gently, he says, *gently*.

I can feel the tickle and burn
of light and dark, heat
and cool, naked
and clothed, a rhythm,
until I want to press down,
to take myself beyond the pulse
of his voice.

Can you hear me?
Can you hear me? Are you there?

I stop. We are waiting now
for the end of things, my body
is uncertain — I want to hear
him guide me over the hesitation.

Do you ever forget your name?

By now I have forgotten my name;
there are so many names
where that one used to be.

He does not know
that I wear six different names
each night before the bleary
mornings come. I reach inside me
hoping to push back that first name
so far that come daylight
it will be gone for good.

After, in the hiatus,
I hear more paper.

Then, as if to someone else:
Goodnight, ladies, goodnight, sweet ladies, goodnight, goodnight.

HAVE MERCY!

The clean line of a preacher's suit
as he struts about on the red carpet—

this black man of power—the rolls
of skin at the back of his shaven head,

the thick fat hands, the way his slacks
stretch over his pert ass, the way

he turns it to the nodding congregation,
the way he does his little dance,

and the close-up of his lips,
his tongue reaching to moisten

the corners of his mouth,
the sweat, the body leaning forward,

all this with the television mute
fills my eyes with just what I need

to turn this white man's voice,
grunting out his quick orgasm

in my ears, hoping I too am imagining
him as he says he is—the lies we tell.

I come hiccupping to the soft shoe
of the preacher's holy delight, gasping,

Jesus, Jesus, Jesus, have mercy on me!

FLASHER

He calls me an emotional flasher;
the neurosis of the logic
that others would like to see
my vulnerable bareness
in glorified pathetic splendor
arrests me. I laugh but consider
the truth of this — consider why he,
a stranger beside me thousands
of feet above the Atlantic,
smiles in that come-on way
he has mastered after fifty years,
to say, *Come on, you can*
tell me; you won't see me again —
I won't tell your husband.
I am laughing stupidly.
And then I flash.

                    I can smell him.

SKIN

My skin is as readable as my heart:
transparent—it hides nothing of my history—
leaves a narrative of contradictory omens
and I sweat when I see him,
fighting for the casual; it does not come
easy—I am horny today, and I brush
against him every chance I get. My skin
is a map of blotches where the sun
and the allergies of his presence make me
break out. He is reading my secrets
etched in, like henna, across my back,
tracing the lines like they are brail;
I shiver at his touch. We are listening
to the music of lost things, the things
I would rather forget, which I breathe
to the tracing of his fingers along my back.
My orgasm was such a wretched howl
and I swooned quickly into sleep,
thinking of today when I would show
him what my husband has done to me.
He whispers into my hair,

Are these marks

from my fingers, my compositions,
these fresh ones, or are they his
that you have brought to show me
that when you leave this place,

you make your own stories,
writing me out of your world?

It feels as if he is ready to run again,
and I hold him, tell him that at night
I imagine him over me, his voice
urging me into the sublimation
of desire — that I always think
of him. He is silent, his hands
start to move again, and these undulations
on my skin are the watering down
of memory, the fading of blood.

Mark me, press your nails in me,
make me bleed, write into
this girl's skin the hieroglyphs
of your ownership, then tongue
and blow the skin until your brand
is in me for as long as we live.

I am sweating again, my body falls
softly forward, and in this place
I drift into a damp sleep, listening
to his low humming to the warm
bass of the music under us.

LANGUAGE

At first there is the stirring on the edge
of dream, the taste of sleep, and the bitter
residue of night still in the mouth,
before the sharp cut of that early light,
a ladder of glow through the pinking lattice work.
I think of Spanish words, they form
in the mind like a dream I have had,
no meaning in this crawl of Spanish words
in chalk on green slate — my brain
will not make it live — it sits there,
the panic of not knowing weighing on me;
the man I have found on the chat line
has given me his number, and I can tell
by the way he uses words like *apotheosis*
that he is a tender lover, that he reads,
that he understands fantasy, that he will
love me with words and never demand
to touch me, except with words.
I can tell this from the words he uses,
and I like him, perhaps he was in that foggy
dream, tantalizingly distant — he does not speak
Spanish, I know, but he loves words.
He will love these words that keep turning
in my head, and the day of loss
does not happen. Instead, I imagine
the absence: My husband has left

with the children for the day care,
To give me a break, he says, his eyes
filling with tears — I dislike the proprietor
in him, he does not know my hunger.
It has been hours and all I feel
is relief and the pleasant memory
of twilight gleaming on the tops of trees,
like the rebel women I saw on *Nova*
in that documentary of unsteady
cameras, sharp reds and greens —
women carrying long baskets
of coca leaves over dense hillsides,
their cheeks swollen with chewed
leaves, their eyes red, glazed
with the same inertia that comes over
women drunk with too many orgasms
(I want dark drunken eyes like theirs) —
above, the rest of the world a dull blue.
And I can tell by the burn of my
nipples against the silk of my blouse,
and the unfurling of meaning in those
words — *junta, caer, película* — the
constancy of a language so rhythmic
it sounds like music — *mañana, mañana* —
morning, tomorrow, morning, tomorrow —
that I am hungry, that I need to touch words.
I dial his number, listen for a voice,
then begin to softly repeat

this foreign tongue in my head
until he groans, and shouts.

TRANSLATING LOVE

My gray days gather like the delicate eyelets
of my needle's pricks; threaded, each stretch
of fabric is patterned — I love another
so dumbly that I count hours for his voice.

I am learning to say *love* as an unguent
for the tawdriness of our coupling
in rank motels, in the darkness under
the back stairs — fumbling for flesh,

swallowing the groan — leaving behind
the condom wrapped in tissue. To return
each night, I call it love, make an epic
of it, imagine desire in poems and songs.

Prayer comes easy in this small room;
I fall to the floor and tears seep — it is hard
not to cry; the heavy gloom of my chest —
that he will not love me is my terror.

Some things are solved. Old crushes crumble,
turn to powder in the face of this. I know
the dialect of my desire now — my woman's
blood warms to a simple metaphor: lust.

In three days the walls will melt,

I will smell of blood; I will weep more,
the taut muscle of my desire will grow liquid;
I will take long baths to soothe the weary nerves.

I know seasons, the come and go of need.
I will carry this as a talisman of possibility.
Winter is crawling over the plains. The scarecrows
are infested by ravens; the corn is blighted.

Give me the memory of that smoked studio
where the skinny brown man with a head too large
for his shoulders skanked out a nation's pain.
I was there, nurturing the dubplate of desire.

This love is green as the St. Mary hills where the rivers
are swift, the soil black, the sky full with daily rain.
This love is mellow as a Culture tune, harmonies
undulating in the mango groves, pungent and damp.

Outside it is gray, and my music floats
here like oil on water—a glittering skin
of rainbows. It is morning, my stomach hurts,
I want you to call; to whisper me to sleep.

THE PROPHET'S WIFE

Go, take to yourself an adulterous wife and children of
unfaithfulness, because the land is guilty of the vilest
adultery in departing from the LORD.   —Hosea 1:2

My sin is biblical—I am the wife of the prophet,
though my man's holiness is merely a product of contrasts.

Still, remember the whore who the prophet found,
cleaned up, and brought to his marriage tent;

the one who after a few days felt the stirrings
in her belly and went out? Remember her?

They called her *whore* for want of words to speak
to the insatiable hunger of her desire, the wantonness

of her waywardness. But whores are less venal;
their sin is mammon and the calculation

of economics of need. Me, I am like the prophet's
wife, the one who kept a record of the shape

of every penis she met—the one who wakes
early and crawls into the street to give herself

to the thirst of fools. I have nothing to show
for this but the biblical proportion of my flaming.

II

Rock Hill, South Carolina, 2004

She will chase after her lovers but not catch them;
she will look for them but not find them.
Then she will say,
I will go back to my husband as at first,
for then I was better off than now.

—Hosea 2:7

AGAINST CARNALITY

You asked me to incant life
    a lyric of hope.

Yet all I speak are narratives
    of consuming flesh.

Teach me the language of life,
    a dancing song, oh Spirit.

THE CONVENIENCE OF MERCY

He knows that what he imagines
is gentler than what he would hear
were I to confess it all, breathlessly.

He knows that in his nightmares
I still have the tender wisdom
of a mother, the grace of a wife,
the wounded hunger of a child;
and my words are always pure
despite the slipperiness of my ways.

He knows we forgive only the things
we know, the rest is God's affair.

HINTERLAND

Georgetown, Guyana, 2000

Further inland, beyond the dank stench
of old soap, shed skin, and spilt piss

in the gangrened gutters, algae-
green in the rich fluorescent way

of rot, elemental rot; beyond the tar-
stained dykes along the indifferent beach,

beyond the stretch of cornfields,
a horizon of green spears scratching

the startling sky, blue, big, so wide,
the hills are small lumps undulating

along the bias of the wide
windscreen of this bus. At dusk

the darkness was sudden, the trees
crawling closer to the damp road,

whispering the disquiet of breezes.
So deep inside this land, the twist

of roads, this entanglement of river
and jungle, we arrived at a clearing,

the ground, brilliant white sand
in the moon glow, as if God began

the beach here, then changed his mind,
leaving the shells, dunes, and brittle

sand among the chattering trees,
thick-trunked and wide as houses.

In this place, where the rain came
nightly, thundering on the zinc roof

of the mess hall, we took shelter
under the dripping eaves, and we looked

into the inscrutable dialogue of the night
and poured our stories out, softly, softly.

HUSBAND

Peach oil soap in yellow plastic bowls.
You wash for an hour until your skin puckers
and everything is soft on you, rubbery
to touch. You wipe yourself as if for the first
time, then slip beside him bare as forgiveness.

What makes a man pull you close
after he has waited those hours for you
to wander in off the wet streets, after
the roads have grown silent, and he has
rehearsed his weeping at the news of your death?

How does he whisper love to you,
when you cannot tell if the damp in you
is from the shower, his ministrations,
or the leavings of that ghost in the shadows?

You come with tears and trembling,
you come with tears and trembling.

CERTIFIED

I have been certified—the news is good.
Now I can draw a line for memory's sake.
Before the ritual of pills, the assurance of dogma,
there was little else but to imagine
a woman's poor self-control, a horny
skettel falling back to old haunts
after each lengthy repentance.

Now I can draw a line for memory's sake.
Everything has slowed now,
my body has grown fatter—these drugs
make you hungry for the comfort of food—
and the nervous twitch is gone.
I swear the puffiness has eased
in my vagina—no longer am I
that pink-assed Barbary monkey
turning up her stuff at all the males
scattered through the savannah.

I have been certified—the news is good.
Call me mad, call the riot in my blood
the chemistry of desire, call it something
that makes me know the woman
hurtling through the night to find
a man with a dick in his hand,
to kneel so he could push it in,

to wait to hear him sigh his arrival,
to hope he would say *love*, as if love
was a word he invented for her — I know this
to be pure madness, and I embrace it —
the madness, that is. I embrace my madness.

Now I draw a line for memory's sake.
Today I start counting my days.
The trees have shed everything now.
The snow will come next.
I have not forgotten much;
it is just the promise of that line
of hope, that calmer place, that peace
beyond which lies a safer country.

THE COURTYARD

We found a courtyard in this rented home
here in the outskirts of the city where black birds
line the wires sagging beside unbroken fields
and the concrete has spread like the stony skin
of a man paralyzed by a stroke—so much white
concrete, identical buildings, and lives of such
middle-class order. We found this green
courtyard, a hidden thing tucked into the corner
of our home that abuts a forest. Someone planted
wild flowers and built trestles for grape vines
to grow untamed. They poured pink marl
swirled into raw concrete in pools on the grass,
pools that never grow hot for the shade of apple
trees, nor too cold in the early thaw, for the dappled
warmth of sunlight filters through the tangle of branches.
Here, we sit at dusk, closed in by the tall fence,
listening to the hum of insects, and we drink
a bottle of simple wine, silently staring
at the way that the rose of the bottle looks
like blood on the wooden table. It is easy
to forget the squalor of those years beyond
the thick bramble and bushes, beyond the green
of this shelter. You read your books,
I talk of the genus of roses and the notes
I have been taking about fermenting grapes
and drying fruit; and sometimes I tell you

of the antique shop at the corner of our lane
where I have secreted in a dark corner
three eighteenth-century gardening guides,
hoping one day to slip them away. We laugh
as if we have already grown old and tender,
as if we have arrived at those years of grace
when all sins have been forgiven, or at least
faded into the wisdom of our now pliant hearts.

TIMES SEVEN

The woman coming through the trees,
the speckled light of dusk

on her skin, is your love
returning again to be forgiven

with tears in her face;
embrace the broken woman.

WHAT WE HAVE LEARNED

1

We have learned not to keep a tally
of the numbers we make up.

We never share the names we have invented
for who we are: the wounded,
the spoiled, the uncared for,
the unloved, the broken,
the shattered, the scarred,
the holes, the holes, the holes.

These we keep secret: Naming, counting,
calculating the havoc caused
or the weight of hatred we could carry
is more than anyone should bear.

Still we know the story—there is comfort
in the lines we can draw from
this calm capacity to spread ourselves
on floors, broken beds, stained sofas,
filthy yards, battered car seats—
spread ourselves to be taken
surreptitiously in the dark.

How easily we recover to ourselves,
never doubting for a moment

what grace is — we know grace.

All creatures caught in their squalor
know the language of purity;
its gentle hand washing away
the caking of our filth — we know this
well and give thanks for mercies.

2

Our insanities are quiet things.
They arrive in pragmatic calculations,
and we have learned to speak them
in those dark moments when our needs
overwhelm us: *You too will hurt
me, and I will let you hurt me,
and you will think you have ruled me,
but you will never understand
that I have forgotten the rituals
of hurt — now they come as ordinary
paths to my peace*. We have learned
to carry in us the bloom of desire,
a kind of perverse daring that we break
loose in dark rooms, frightening
our lovers with the unfolding
of ourselves. What they won't know
is that each orgasm is a triumph,
each lilting arrival, a prayer

against the rotting of the body;
each little death is a revival,
a kind of sacrament against
the days of such gloom
when we could not fathom
beauty in us, could not turn
our broken bodies into songs,
could not laugh constantly
without the haunting of its ending
looming over us. Our lovers
may not know that sometimes
we shout to deafen the echo
of some lewd urging — something
that belongs to another memory;
that in mid-coitus or in some casual
instance by a tree or a stove,
something spoken can still
in us the ordinary language
of living. We have learned
never to pull the meaning
of our hesitation, our scream,
our sudden freezing into the open.

3
We have learned silence. We know
the story of our unmaking.
We will not tell it easily,

never to explain anything
except the anger that lights
in our heads, making us scratch
our scalps violently; except
the way we can grow distant,
leaving everything behind;
except the loudness of our pleasure,
the way we howl our sweetness.

4

I will offer only the general facts,
nothing of the detail.
The horror in that is more
than words would allow —
after all, there is a glazed eye
in all of us — some infant child
who has vowed never to speak
again. For her, I too have lost
words. I offer only this:
that my three brothers
and a cluster of friends
raped my ten-year-old body.

SWEET OLD WOMEN

A woman wants to sit on the edge of the city
waiting for the young girls to gather at her feet,
to learn the pattern of grass weaved into baskets
or the secret of the sweet aftertaste in the stew —
and she says loudly, *I just stick my foot in and stir,*
which is enough for a day of reverence when age
is a balm over all sins. Just sometimes, one will come
by with tears or the lament of some bruised love
in her — the weight of guilt on her chest, a girl
full of questions about the taste of love, the one
who asks why people don't just fall dead rather
than carry the stone in their chest of love.
Sometimes she sits her down, and they watch
the way the light falls across the street,
the shadows growing long — and in this silence
she chuckles a deep sweetness that grows
into an open-faced laugh, which is wrong
in this time of mourning, but even the girl
must giggle, wiping her face to hide her teeth,
staring back with this question, as if this woman
spread to spilling on her stool has now, at last,
lost her mind.
          But mad women will speak;
old mad women will unfurl the stories they carry
inside them, the stories that have been hiding,
even as they have danced in their heads,

made their skins tingle, made their soft chuckles
bubble out at funerals, at wakes, at the bedside
of some dying soul. Old mad women, if you ask,
will tell you of the secrets they cherish, the men
they have held hostage to their hips in the green
grotto behind the cemetery, the men who wept
to learn of other lovers, the men who crumbled
when their penises remained flaccid, useless,
despite the boasts, the promises, or men who have
turned them into soft flowers, then torn them
petal by petal into the bacchanal of desire, howling,
howling; men who have made them wake late at night
to walk through damp fields smelling out
the hunger of their lusts; and women who touched
them so tenderly, that in their arrivals in those
hidden rooms where women sew frocks,
burn hair, and share the whisperings of the wounds
they have born—there in those menthol-
scented rooms, they felt their skins turned
inside out, their eyes falling deep into gloom,
when they lost the meaning of words
for the first time, for the only time;
when, in the panting nervy heat of the after-
math, they promised never to speak of this,
but always to carry its memory in them;
so that even now, when they think of a name
like Lucy or Merle or Eartha or Una,
they still feel the dew of desire in their vaginas.

Old mad women carry these things and more
in them, and if pushed, if goaded, they will
hum a hymn and then tell of the meaning
of desire. A woman wants to grow old
like such women, the protectors of the gate.
Women who will make even the most wayward
of women understand that the longing
in them, the taste for sweetness on those days
when the blood is gathered deep in them,
is the promise of God, and laughter
is the healing, and memories lengthen days
when they are warm with such thick
pleasures. A woman wants to collect
her secrets so she can have dreams
when the days grow darker and cool.
A woman wants to age like these sweet
old women, copious bosoms full of a hundred
embraces, and laughter wide enough
to ease the broken — women with memories
that do not canker but continue to bloom
into fresher and fresher flowers.

WATER CARRIER

For my husband, the prophet

I carry water in cupped hands,
I have found a thirsty lip,
I pour, he drinks quickly,
his throat rolling, his eyes grateful.

I dip again, he is waiting,
I feel the soft of his lip
flame my fingertips.

His tongue cleans my palm.
He makes water with his eyes,
beckons me to taste the salt.

I am the water carrier.
I feel the livid sweetness
of my giving, and the bright
alertness of this salt
touching my tongue.

END OF THE AFFAIR

I hate the word *deploy*
let's use *use*, although I am sending
and sending these lies to you,

but not sending but letting them go
in what I am not saying,
and waiting for the end of things,

though I know the end of things
and fear are the bridge I slide on,
waiting for you to stare at me,

cold as stone, asking me what,
after all is said and done, is the ploy.

WHY A WOMAN GOES LOW-RIDING

The fourth day, I wrote words
that returned to me void. I watched
the sleepers: my son, his tender mouth
still pulling at a nipple that smarts —
the piercing draw that burns
the nape of my neck;
my daughter, her dreams floating
over her clean as clouds, how
they carry their days; and my husband,
my saint, whose arms twitch, the clean
tendons tasting the electric aftershocks
of his day with the dumbbells —
I watch them unable to face the golden
swoop of a camera over these fields
that turn around a city about to crumble.
I am among the flame and ruin,
the howls and screams, the blue-green
glass blackened and crushed, the sirens,
my children, where are my children?
My bleeding hands, the gash in my head,
the terror of that black falling cloud,
the thin veneer of cement dust on my
tongue, my children, where are my broken
children? One crushed on an old desk,
the other strewn in even bits — I am
stumbling in this bloody swirl

and it is all leaving me. My love,
you should be here to see the madness
in my eyes, my dumb lip quivering,
the large growth on my stomach —
this pregnancy of pus and the substance
of horror. But you left me to myself
and I see the room again, hating you,
your cold logic, your stoic, sensible care.

SECRET

I horde these secrets,
they come each day;
I remember the time
in another life, unfolding
the letters of my beloved
and eating his secrets,
my heart rushing.

It is true that I never hold secrets
long; I camouflage them in words,
then push them out into the bush;
I reheat the secrets passed on to me
by friends who know my ways.

Now I grow cynical
(read *wise, honest*)
knowing that these secrets
are fictions to be told;
I tell them ruthlessly,
my heart rushing,
rushing away from me.

PRETENDER

There are those who have discovered
the simple grace of pre-confession,
like writers devoted to inertia
who repeat the brilliant plots
of their *in vitro* creations at cocktail
gatherings, jinxing the things to inaction;
plots conjured then forgotten.

My friend tells me the evidence
of could-be infidelities, exposing
herself generously with laughter,
spoiling the pleasure of secretive lusts.
And she stays faithful, though
dressed like a flaming adulteress.

Me, I secret my sins against the day
when the lies will blossom,
strewn gloriously, lewdly
on the off-white sheets, the words
entwined like bodies, twisted
in pure assured action.

PEACH BEER

After the hysterectomy

I can see the pinking age of my womb—
it has been years, a lifetime—I see its contours
for the first time, and it all seems familiar,
an odd homecoming despite the metal probe
with its impersonal eye obeying the short-breathed
expletives of the doctor. Beyond this,
there is little soul-searching left.

The ritual of bloodletting is over: The ovaries,
now weary, are a liability, they will go.
He does not understand the rupture, its meaning.
He reads something like freedom.
A stainless steel pan with purple
and deep mauve sacs, blood, and gangrene.
There will be a hole—emptiness.

Outside, the city's traffic has slowed
to a drunken slouch under the soft deep orange
of dusk—and the green of this piedmont,
the last preening of the dogwood
is turning golden in the muting light.
I pull off the road, beneath a shedding gingko,
and dial for a voice, a simple voice
with music and the collected memory
of a lost, forgivable indiscretion: a cool

room, the slow groan of jive, the feel
of a body guiding me through the tears —
how he made me feel graceful again.

I listen to the laughter of recognition,
feel the flooding of that terminal womb,
the slower ovaries making for the last,
the musky concoction of peach beer.
I smell the salt of fresh blood,
the musk of my desire, the bouquet
of my sap, still full in the golden air.

This warmth, this precious sunlight,
touches my nipples, turns my head
into a flambeaux, makes my skin
grin, makes me grow another inch.
This farewell seems forever, the soft
swallow of his tears, the embarrassed
giggle, the hum of remembrance, the song
he sings in a voice cracked with the
sadness of the act, like praying on the phone.

In the silence after, the sticky
skin all slippery with the proper
funk of desire, I drive home,
stretch out beneath a blighted peach tree
and watch the moon arc and bend
into the space left by the clouds.

THE WOUNDS I HAVE MADE

I still feel the weight of mornings
filled with the bloated sorrows
we carried—the silence over us

after my confessions,
the salt residue of your tears
on my fingers; the tender sorrow

of your eyes, how you wanted
me to hold you, how you felt
me hurt you, how your body

assaulted you with its
twisted language; the cold,
the dry wind, the regret on

our long walk away from
ourselves. This blood in my
hand is always there. How

you forgave me, how you
still loved me beyond that
place; that betrayal.

THE CHEMISTRY IN MY BLOOD

These seasons return, I ignore the code
tapping in my flesh—still I have ritualized
the slackening of the gate, made a prayer
of the rationalizing— *Why would God so curse*
me? I repeat the prescribed scriptures,
my skin burning, my voice slipping
into the memory of desire: his hand, his
slippery hands stained with my secretions.

This thing comes on us in our thirtieth
year, trips our wombs, our eggs
aged but concocting a brew so thick
with its language, dark like the bottom
of a stout keg where the musk of heat
has soured into a potent intoxicant,
makes me go for long walks through parks,
smelling the rising funk under my dress.

After prayer, staring into the evening,
the tide of my blood ebbing,
I calculate the price of sin, draw
lines and numbers banking on the balance,
the periods of dry devotion, then I let
slip, my voice gathered in the crude
discourse of my fantasies—I speak
my way to release—plunging deep

to find the orgasm that will cool me
for good, for a month, a week, a day,
for this dark evening waiting for the babies
to wake, or for you to come home—
sometimes it seems so long
between these emptyings.

Later a sister calls to say in that soft
pitying voice of the holy, *They have called
a fast for tomorrow*, and I hang up,
curled into myself, and tremble
before the Lord, so heavy am I
with the fall of my blood, the syrup
of my chemistry—I too must call a fast.

CYCLE

The season of blood
has passed.

Now is the season
of wariness.

Soon, the season
of silence.

Then the new season
of blood.

I wait for a break
in the sky.

III

Cassava Piece, Kingston, 1977

So I bought her for fifteen shekels of silver and about a homer and a lethek of barley. Then I told her, You are to live with me many days; you must not be a prostitute or be intimate with any man, and I will live with you.

—Hosea 3:2, 3:3

WHERE ARE THE ANGELS?

A girl sees a boy with long legs like tree trunks
and a body, wiry, that moves like water
when sweated — a body now turning with dark
new growth in armpits and crotch; a voice
broken into the deep brownness of manhood;
sees that body bent over a daft mongrel,
tongue hanging, eyes darting about — a bitch
anxious for the seeding of her heat —
bent over, pushing into this squatted dog,
that voice like crushed pebbles barking,
the body humping before the long
prayer to Jesus, the limp arms, the bewildered
beast hopping away, sniffing the corners
of the zinc fence, looking back at this boy,
wiping himself while searching about
for witnesses. What darkness enters
the eyes of a girl, peeping through
the slats in the old door of the toilet,
her bowels opening up at the sight,
her heart hopping for the fear of being seen,
for the sweet upheaval in her belly;
where are the angels in the ackee tree
to ward off the shadow that grows in her?

SWEET AND DANDY

I learned the acrobatics of the waistline
before I knew the healing of a slow grind.

Toots and the Maytals are chanting
Sweet and Dandy, and in the dusty
backyard I hold my hands against
my bony chest and roll my backside
like a tutored whore, and the people
know I have a gene of desire in me —
they do not caution or judge, but stare
with the awe and pity of people
seeing a newly born two-headed cow.

My brother is lying in the dark house
alone. The machete wound is dry now,
but they could not fix his left eye
so it would close. If I close my eyes
and think of the slip of my pelvis
and the way my thighs open and close,
and let the music pulse through me,
I can forget the screaming of my mother,
drunk, stretched out, her feet kicking
in the dust and the almond leaves,
holding her chest, wailing for her son.

FATHER

What to make of a man
in his baggy khaki suit
he's been wearing for forty years
taking a rum in a bar,
who hears me coming
without looking, and is told,
See yuh dawta, here,
by Millicent the broken-down
bartender; a man who laughs
and turns with open arms,
his dark broken teeth glowing,
his face a crumpled
and oil-stained brown
paper bag; who I adore
despite every cruelty;
who opens his arms
like a dream he knows
I have had all my life,
and says, *Come, dawta;*
then when I am close,
close enough to smell
the rum in his skin,
pulls his arms in,
embraces himself,
giggling,
What yuh want,

magga gial?
Talk quick?

PEACE

He returns at night with machete
and the thick syrup of rum
clogs my breathing. The taste of fear,
the sign of loathing — regret
is the music behind the image:
this aria of searing loss.
Alone with him I see his eyes,
his mouth moving, no words,
but the gloss of penitence, pleading
for a hand on his battered head
to say, *Released, released*;
I stare, then withdraw, cold air
on my skin. The machete
comes over me. Some die in
dreams. I want to gather my
trembling self in a soft place —
calming the bitterness
of loss; the burden of his shame;
want to warm myself with a wash
of grace, the way God's love falls
upon us, sweetly, simply.
But these sliding songs are all
I have in me, all I can give,
my voice turning about in the dark.
It is three in the morning.
The lights are dull on my skin.

I will hear my voice praying,

Peace, peace, peace, peace!

LONG TIME

... do you, do you, think about that?
—Bob Marley

Long time I don't see a morning
electric like a dream what turn out
not to be a dream beat up 'gainst sleep all night,

or a morning fresh like a rhythm guitar
calling in sun is shining with a fat bass
humming righteousness to the soul

like how some poem when you read it first
leave you with salt in your mouth,
frighten you how things ease back.

Long, long time I don't hear a music
could make me think that I don't know,
yet I know how it fit with light.

Want to rub up 'gainst a music,
make it carry me through dew wetness
of Mannings Hill, make me find peace

like logwood burning, the taste
of roast breadfruit and cool slice pear
and a sweet hot cocoa tea.

AFTER LOVE

On the first day, the day I lay
stretched out in the dull sunlight,
my body betraying me with moistness,
I confessed my love to you
in the language of a timid starved child.
My father came to me with a machete,
the room smelling sweet with rum
and the mugginess of his day-old sweat —
and the windows shattered, we were
all cowering, my mother's graying locks
twisting like a fairy-tale entanglement
of vines through the room, something
like roots, and he hacked at them
until they bled and I stood with
a cornfield of shocked stumps,
my voice hoarse and my heart
growing a second skin. He came
through the door again and again,
and asked me to touch his head,
the heat being too much for him,
it did not end calmly, the blood,
the chunks of knotted hair, the heavy
scent of weed, the way I felt
myself dying quickly, my breath
going, and I screamed, clutching
at my womb; the light in the hall

slicing the darkness. He slept
and you were far away thinking
about how I said I loved you
after telling you the story, or not.

FOR MY DEAD LOVER

I fear sleep and the vengeance
of a father too used to these resurrections.
My eyes are pretty now—bloodshot:
I have not eaten in two days; the drone
of his voice haunting me. I stay
awake, sitting in the clean pool of light
from the stark hanging lamp, counting
my pennies—sack after sack, a ritual
of mythmaking; trying to conjure
the dream of him and me standing
beneath a shedding poui tree, the taste
of reggae in our mouths like the after-
sour of a too strong mint, not touching,
our words floating in the withering
yellow of these poui petals, the grace
of their anointing—this light filling
me, like light fills the nyabinghi's
head while he spins, all billowing
cloth and riotous locks on the foot-
hardened trumping place of groundings.
He is in my skin. I can't sleep.
My husband snores softly, so far from
me, so oblivious to the quarrel
of my febrile days. The sun grows.
It has been three days since the news
of your painful death, my love,

and still the dreams continue
in my head, you still help me
to sweet orgasms and tears.
I am grateful, my love,
that you have not left me, amen.

RITUALS

The lessons you will whisper about love:
the constant habitual kindnesses,
they turn into sacrifices—
some truths are irrevocable: the familiar
rituals of affection; the terror of losing
a limb—we cherish these grotesque arms,
these fingers, stumpy, pale, with splintered
nails; we grow to love their wrinkled
tributaries, too long our own, this love
we keep and toast the years for how
long we have lasted—this too is love.

But the touchstone of love, the thing
it does not have to be, is the pebble
you have kept, smooth, and wrapped in the purple
old J.O.S. bus ticket, fifty cents
to take you to him at sunset, to stand
in the street and share the truth of your life,
this memory of tears, the returning pang
of loss, the familiar smile, the sin
in sometimes, just sometimes, dreaming
of his body against you—the flaming myth,
despite the impossibility of it all—the
scrawled inscription: *For you, my friend,*
who are teaching me the language of love.

News comes. He is dead. The passing
was terrible—he suffered. Your tears
swell—in the darkness, even if it has been
twenty-five years of silence. And still,
your husband's hand reaches to hold you,
to comfort you with familiar love.

PUNISHMENT

Rock Hill, South Carolina, January 2005

I welcome the chastisement.
I have stood under the healing shadows,
felt the hand of mercy — I don't receive it easily.

Then walking away I stumble. Hard to believe
that I have discarded it all at the altar,
and now upright, I can walk away

like one having picked up a bargain,
pocket none the lighter. I have
cheated the salesperson who is caught

in the prison of her promises. I have long known
the wages of my sin; I have understood
the whip, the fruit of failure. To walk

away now bloodless, unburdened,
forgiven, seems patently decadent,
and I keep looking around, waiting

for the fire to fall. Perhaps it is
the uncertainty, the long wait for the curse
to come upon me, that is my punishment:

the secret cancer, the tragic accident,

the revelation of divorce, the death
of a child, blindness, a disease

in my vagina, long dormant,
now awakening just when I think
I know the peace of God;

these things looming over me,
waiting to overtake me
when I have relaxed a little.

Still I battle my appetite with fasts
and carry the weight of guilt on me.
But this is not freedom, not the birthright

of bloodshed and broken flesh.
I receive the bargain of the ages and turn
to face my fragile collateral:

the husband, the children, these words,
still intact, still within my reach —
against this debt I cannot repay.

BIRDS IN THE CHIMNEY

Rock Hill, South Carolina, March 2005

The birds are back in the chimney
dropping dead insects. Morning
filters in the rituals of spring,
a lullaby for bleary-eyed women.

I have dreamed the sheltering
of my wounded self inside
a yellow Volkswagen, the converging
of history and dream—an equation
for nightmares. This pulpy, pulsing
flesh, the slovenly girl punished
for leaving the billowing sheets
out in the dusty air, night falling.

How they beat me: love and monstrosity,
the air reeking of rum, the blood
of my period, the stench of wretchedness.

It is hard to sleep, counting the hours—
the reels of old films unraveling.
I know the faces of the men
who have taken me again
and again: I need professional help,
sweet Savior. I was born for this story.

The light burns my eyes. Outside, the flash
of white, the flopping sheltering
of those sheets, glowing over the grass,
left out to dry. My heart murmurs
at the sight of my neglected child's
face caked with egg yolk.

But the house is silent, comfortably
accepting my slippage,
and the smell of my baby's sleep fills
the room, the bickering birds calming.

These soft mornings, blood turns blue
        in my hands.

Other selections in Chris Abani's Black Goat poetry series

AUTO MECHANIC'S DAUGHTER
poems by Karen Harryman
84 pages, trade paperback original, $14.95

Charting the vicissitudes of her own life, and the travails and triumphs of the lives of those whom she knows and loves, Harryman's poems travel great distances, both internally and geographically, from the Kentucky of her youth to the California of her present moment (with a detour in Europe). *Auto Mechanic's Daughter* is a lyrical journey into life's private places and the small joys encountered there.

EEL ON REEF poems by Uche Nduka
152 pages, trade paperback original, $15.95

Award-winning Uche Nduka challenges every expectation of an African poet. His unique voice is a heady amalgam of Christopher Okibo, A.R. Ammons, John Ashbery, Kamau Brathwaite, and something only Uche can bring. In reading Nduka's poetry, the reader is encouraged to enjoy each instant, each image, while resisting the instinct to construct linear meaning in the poems.

Also Available from Akashic Books

SHE'S GONE by Kwame Dawes
340 pages, trade paperback original, $15.95

"Dawes offers vibrant characters and locales, from Jamaica to the American South to the Urban North, in this diaspora of black culture and strong emotions, bordering the fine line between love and madness between two troubled people."
—*Booklist*

SONG FOR NIGHT by Chris Abani
164 pages, trade paperback original, $12.95

"Chris Abani might be the most courageous writer working right now. There is no subject matter he finds daunting, no challenge he fears. Aside from that, he's stunningly prolific and writes like an angel. If you want to get at the molten heart of contemporary fiction, Abani is the starting point."
—**Dave Eggers,** author of *What Is the What*

"Not since Jerzy Kosinski's *The Painted Bird* or Agota Kristof's Notebook Trilogy has there been such a harrowing novel about what it's like to be a young person in a war. That Chris Abani is able to find humanity, mercy, and even, yes, forgiveness, amid such devastation is something of a miracle."
—**Rebecca Brown,** author of *The End of Youth*